Tom and Ricky

and the

Man With the Red Hair

High Noon Books
Novato, California

Cover Design: Nancy Peach
Interior Illustrations: Herb Heidinger

Glossary: job, carts, tire, shopping, soup, store, eyes, twins

International Standard Book Number: 0-87879-358-5

9 8 7 6 5 4
5 4 3 2 1 0 9 8

Contents

CHAPTER 1

A Broken Bike

Tom stopped his bike. He was right in front of Ricky's house. Ricky was sitting out in front.

"What's doing?" Tom called out.

"Not too much," Ricky answered.

"Want to go somewhere?" Tom asked.

"I can't," Ricky answered.

"Why not?" Tom asked.

"My bike," Ricky said.

"Your bike? What's up?" Tom asked.

"It's broken," Ricky answered.

1

"Not again. What did you do?" Tom asked.

"I was riding with Eddie. I went over a small hill. Patches got in the way. You should see it," Ricky said.

"Let's take a look at it. Maybe I can help fix it," Tom said.

"It's in the back. Come," Ricky said.

Tom and Ricky went around the house. The bike was there. Tom looked at the bike.

"I see what you mean," Tom said.

"I think I need another bike," Ricky said.

"I think you do, too," Tom said.

"Let's go down to Mr. Ward. He might have a good used bike at his store," Ricky said.

"That's a good idea. Come on," Tom said.

Ricky got on Tom's bike. Patches started to bark. "No, Patches. You stay. We'll be right back," Ricky said.

Patches walked back to the house. He looked sad as the boys went to Front Street.

"Mr. Ward has a lot of good bikes. He'll have a good used bike," Tom said.

Tom stopped his bike in front of Mr. Ward's bike store. They both went inside.

"Can I help you boys?" Mr. Ward said.

"I need to buy a bike," Ricky said.

"I just got some new ones," Mr. Ward said.

"I want to buy a used dirt bike," Ricky said.

"I have some good used ones. Look at these," Mr. Ward said.

Tom and Ricky walked over to the used bikes. There were five.

"These look OK," Tom said.

"How much is the red one?" Ricky asked.

"That's the best one I have. It's $45," Mr. Ward said.

"$45?" Ricky asked.

"Yes. That's a good buy. The boy who owned it took good care of it. I didn't have to do much work on it," Mr. Ward said.

"Where are you going to get $45?" Tom asked.

"I don't know," Ricky said.

"You need to get a job," Mr. Ward said.

"I'd like to. But where?" Ricky asked.

"Why don't you try Mr. King? He was in here. He said he needed someone to help him out at his store," Mr. Ward said.

"You're kidding," Ricky said.

"No. Why don't you go over to see him? Maybe the job is still open," Mr. Ward said.

"Come on, Ricky. Let's get over there," Tom said.

"Don't sell that bike, Mr. Ward. I'm going to buy it," Ricky called out.

"I'll keep it for you for a week," Mr. Ward said.

Ricky got on Tom's bike. They started off for Mr. King's store.

CHAPTER 2

The Man With the Red Hair

Ricky got on the back of Tom's bike. Tom went as fast as he could. They both wanted to get to Mr. King's store right away.

"Hurry up," Ricky said.

"I'm going as fast as I can," Tom said.

They got to the store. Ricky jumped off the bike. Then he ran in.

Mr. King was busy. He saw Ricky. He could tell that Ricky wanted to see him.

"Do you need something?" Mr. King asked.

"Well, yes," Ricky answered.

"What is it?" Mr. King asked.

"I'd like a job," Ricky said.

"I'm busy right now. Can you wait?" Mr. King asked.

"Sure I can. I'll wait outside," Ricky said.

Tom was waiting for Ricky. "What did Mr. King say? Did you get the job?" Tom asked.

"Mr. King was busy. There are a lot of people in the store. He said to wait," Ricky answered.

"Let's stay right by the door," Tom said.

"That's a good idea," Ricky said.

A man with red hair and a red shirt was by the door. He kept looking at Tom and Ricky.

"Do you know him?" Tom asked.

"No. I thought you did," Ricky answered.

"What's Mr. King doing?" Tom asked.

A man with red hair and a red shirt was by the door.
He kept looking at Tom and Ricky.

"This is Saturday. A lot of people are in there. Mr. King is helping them find what they need. We just have to wait. Look at all the cars out there," Ricky said.

A lot of people were going in and out of the store. They all had bags full of things.

The man with the red hair and red shirt kept on looking at Tom and Ricky. "Are you waiting for someone?" he asked.

"Yes. We're waiting for Mr. King. He owns the store," Tom said.

"I know that. I've been here before," the man said.

"Are you waiting for someone?" Ricky asked.

"Yes. My friend is in the store. There are too many people in there. I'm waiting for him to come out," the man said.

"Have you been here a long time?" Tom asked.

"Too long," the man said.

"It is a busy day for Mr. King," Ricky said.

All of a sudden a woman came running to the store. She ran inside.

"What was wrong with that woman?" Ricky asked.

"I don't know. She was saying something. It sounded like she said something about the tires on her car," Tom said.

"The tires on her car?" the man asked.

"That's what I thought she said," Tom answered.

"Come on. Let's go in. Let's see what it's all about," Ricky said.

"Maybe we can help her," Tom said.

Then the man said, "I'll go in, too. Maybe I can help."

All three of them went into the store. The woman was talking to Mr. King.

"Now tell me again. Did you say someone took the front tires off your car?" Mr. King asked.

"Yes! Yes! Now I can't move my car," she yelled.

"That just can't be," Mr. King said.

"Well, come and see for yourself," she said.

"And they were new tires!"

Mr. King started to go out with the woman.

"That's him! That's him!" she yelled.

Then she saw the man with the red hair.

"That's him! That's him!" she yelled.

Everyone in the store was looking at the woman.

"What do you mean?" the man said.

"I saw you near my car. You did it," she yelled.

"I couldn't have done it. I have been talking to these boys," the man said.

Mr. King turned to Ricky. "Is that right?" he asked.

"That's right, Mr. King. You told me to wait outside. Tom and I have been talking to him. We have been right by the front door," Ricky answered.

CHAPTER 3

They Both Get A Job

Everyone in the store was looking at the woman. They all wanted to know about her tires. Mr. King knew the woman.

"Don't worry, Mrs. Lake. We'll find out about all of this," Mr. King said.

"Now what do I do? How do I get home?" she asked.

"I'll call Sam at the gas station. I know he will come here. He will put new tires on your car. I will pay for them," Mr. King said.

The woman went back to wait by her car.

"I have to call Sam. I'll be right back," Mr. King said to Tom and Ricky.

Ricky turned to the man with the red hair. "Is your friend still in the store?" he asked.

"I don't see him. He might be outside waiting for me. I think I better go," the man said.

"Do you come here all the time?" Tom asked.

"My friend does. He has a lot of kids. He's always buying food," the man said.

"Maybe we'll see you again. I think I'm going to get a job here," Ricky said.

"My name is Lucky. Maybe I will see you again," the man said. Then he left.

Mr. King came back. "This is funny. Who would take Mrs. Lake's tires?" Mr. King asked.

"Where's that man with the red hair?" Tom asked.

"He just left. He went to meet his friend. They must be in the parking lot," Ricky said.

Tom looked outside the store. "There he is. He is carrying a small bag. He is all by himself. Where is his friend?" Tom asked.

"That doesn't add up. He said his friend was doing a lot of shopping. He'd have more than one small bag," Ricky answered.

"I've never seen him before," Mr. King said.

Then Ricky said, "Mr. King, I need a job. I need to buy a bike. Is there anything I can do?"

"There sure is. A lot of people come here every Saturday. They buy a lot of things. Then they leave the shopping carts in the parking lot. I need someone to bring the carts back into the store. The man who does this for me is sick," Mr. King said.

"I'll do it," Ricky said.

"Do you think you could use two helpers?" Tom asked.

"I think I could. Do you both want a job?" Mr. King asked.

"We sure do," Tom answered.

"Why don't you start right now? Can you?" Mr. King asked.

"We sure can," Ricky said.

"How much will we make?" Tom asked.

"I'll pay you $4 an hour," Mr. King said.

"We each get $4 an hour?" Tom asked.

"That's right," Mr. King answered.

"Oh boy! We can make the money to buy your bike," Tom said.

CHAPTER 4

More Missing Tires

Mr. King showed Tom and Ricky what to do. People put food in the shopping carts. They took the carts to their cars. Then they left the carts in the parking lot.

"Those carts cost me a lot of money. I don't have a lot of them. I need them back in the store for other people to use," Mr. King said.

"OK. We know what to do," Ricky said.

"That's fine. Get the carts back in the store as fast as you can," Mr. King said.

"Boy, this is a big parking lot," Tom said.

"You start over there. I'll start on this side," Ricky said.

"OK. Let's see who can get the most carts," Tom said.

They started to get the carts. They were all over the parking lot. The lot was full of cars.

The boys worked hard. They picked up carts and rolled them into the store. There were always more carts.

Ricky was in back of the parking lot. He saw Lucky walking around.

"Lucky!" he called out.

The man turned. He looked at Ricky. "Who are you calling?" the man asked.

"I was calling you, Lucky," Ricky said.

"I don't know you," the man said.

"Sure you do. Tom and I were talking with you at the front door of the store," Ricky said.

The man looked at Ricky. Then he said, "Oh, that's right. Well, I have to go now." Then he walked away.

Ricky pushed the carts back to the store. He saw Tom coming out of the store. "You know what? I just saw Lucky. I thought he went home," Ricky said.

"You saw Lucky? I just saw him in the store," Tom said.

"In the store? It couldn't have been Lucky. He was just out here," Ricky said.

"No, it was Lucky. He said he needed one more thing for his friend," Tom answered.

"I don't get it," Ricky said.

Just then a man went running into the store. He looked mad.

"Well, maybe he just walks fast," Tom said.

"Could be," Ricky said.

Just then a man went running into the store. He looked mad.

"What's up?" Ricky asked.

"That man sure looks upset," Tom said.

"I have to get these carts into the store," Ricky said.

"I better get going. There are lots more carts out there," Tom said.

Ricky took his carts into the store. He saw the man talking to Mr. King.

"Come over here," Mr. King called to Ricky.

"Do you need me for something?" Ricky asked.

"This man says someone took one of his tires off his car. He says it was done when he was shopping," Mr. King said.

"More tires missing?" Ricky asked.

The man turned to Ricky. "More tires? What does that mean?" he asked.

"Mrs. Lake had two tires taken off her car," Mr. King said.

"Now what do I do?" the man asked.

"I'll help you put your other tire on," Ricky said.

"That will be a big help to me," the man said.

"I'll be out right away," Ricky said.

The man went out to his car.

Then Mr. King asked Ricky, "Did you see anything funny going on in the parking lot?"

"I just saw a lot of people going into the store. And a lot were coming out," Ricky said.

"Is that all you saw?" Mr. King asked.

"Well, let's see. I did see Lucky again," Ricky said.

Just then Lucky walked up to Ricky and Mr. King. "Good to see you again, Ricky," he said.

"I just saw you in the parking lot," Ricky said.

"Not me. I've been in here. Tom saw me here in the store. I needed a can of soup for my friend. He forgot to buy it when he was here before. See? Here it is," Lucky said.

CHAPTER 5

Sergeant Collins Comes By

Ricky ran out into the parking lot. The man was getting a tire out of the trunk of his car.

"Where are you running to?" Tom called out.

"A man had a tire taken off his car. I'm going to help him," Ricky called back.

"Not again," Tom yelled. He was pushing six carts back into the store.

"Yes, again," Ricky called back.

"I just saw Lucky out here in the parking lot," Tom yelled.

"Lucky? I was just talking to him in the store," Ricky said.

Tom left the six shopping carts. He ran back to Ricky. "Wait. I just talked to him over by that red car. Funny, isn't it?" Tom said.

"What's funny?" Ricky asked.

"Red hair, red shirt, and a red car," Tom said.

"That is funny. It's also funny that I saw him in the store. And you saw him out here," Ricky said.

Just then Sergeant Collins came up in his police car. "I saw Sam down at the gas station. He told me you were both working here. How's it going?" the Sergeant asked.

"Fine. It's a lot of work. But I'll have money to buy another dirt bike," Ricky answered.

"Another bike? What's that all about?" the Sergeant asked.

"He busted his bike. We're working here for Mr. King to make some money. That way we can go riding around again," Tom answered.

"Have you seen anything funny going on?" the Sergeant asked.

"Like what?" Ricky asked.

"Sam at the gas station told me about tires being taken," Sergeant Collins said.

"That's right. I am going to help a man right now. He was shopping. A tire was taken off his car," Ricky said.

Just then the man called Ricky. "Are you coming to help me?"

"I'll be right there," Ricky called back.

"You better help that man. I'll talk with Tom. Then I have to go see Mr. King," Sergeant Collins said.

"It sure is busy here. A lot of people are shopping at Mr. King's store," Tom said.

"Have you seen any people just walking around the parking lot?" Sergeant Collins asked.

"You mean people who aren't going shopping?" Tom asked.

"That's right," Sergeant Collins said.

"There's just one man. His name is Lucky," Tom said.

"Is he the only one?" Sergeant Collins asked.

"Yes. But there's something funny about him," Tom said.

"What's funny about him?" the Sergeant asked.

"Well, I see him out here. Ricky sees him in the store. It's almost like he's two people," Tom said.

"Well, that can't be, can it?" the Sergeant said.

CHAPTER 6

The White Car

Tom was talking to Sergeant Collins about Lucky. How could he be in two places at the same time? All of a sudden Tom saw Lucky across the parking lot.

"Look. That's him. He's the man I was talking about," Tom said.

"You mean that man with the red hair?" Sergeant Collins asked.

"Yes. Red hair and a red shirt. And he has a red car," Tom said.

"I see him. But he's over by a white car," Sergeant Collins said.

"That's right," Tom said.

"Look. That's him. He's the man I was talking about," Tom said.

"He looks like he's getting into it," the Sergeant said.

"He sure does," Tom said.

Just then Ricky came back.

"Did you help that man?" Tom asked.

"Yes. We got his other tire on the car. But he was really mad," Ricky said.

"I'm going to go and see Mr. King. You boys keep your eyes open. Let me know if you see anything funny going on," the Sergeant said.

"We sure will," Tom answered.

"We better get back to work," Ricky said.

A woman walked by Ricky. She had two big bags filled with food. "Can you help me?" she asked Ricky.

"I sure can. Where's your car?" he asked as he took the two bags from her.

"It's right over there. It's that white car," she said.

When they got to the car, the woman yelled, "Look! Look at my car. A tire is missing!"

"Stay right here. I'm going to get Sergeant Collins," Ricky said.

The woman didn't move. She stayed right by her car. Ricky went running back to the store. On the way back he saw Tom.

"Come on, Tom. We have to get Sergeant Collins," Ricky called.

"What's up?" Tom called back.

"Another tire is missing," Ricky called back.

34

Tom and Ricky ran into the store.

Sergeant Collins was talking with Mr. King. They saw the boys come running in.

"Don't tell me. Is it another missing tire?" Mr. King asked.

"It sure is," Ricky said.

"What's going on here?" Mr. King asked.

"What car is the tire missing from?" the Sergeant asked.

"It's a white one out in the parking lot," Ricky said.

"I thought so," Sergeant Collins said.

"How did you know that?" Mr. King asked.

"I'll tell you later. Is Lucky here in the store?" Sergeant Collins asked.

"You mean that man with the red hair and the red shirt?" Mr. King asked.

"That's the one," Sergeant Collins answered.

"Yes. I just saw him. He's been in about six times today," Mr. King said.

"Look! There he is over there," Ricky said.

"I think we're going to clear up this mystery right now," the Sergeant said.

CHAPTER 7

A Surprise for Everyone

Sergeant Collins walked over to Lucky. Lucky looked surprised when he saw Sergeant Collins.

"I want to see you. Come with me," the Sergeant said.

"I haven't done anything," Lucky said.

"Just come with me," the Sergeant said.

Sergeant Collins brought Lucky over to Mr. King, Tom, and Ricky. "Is this the man you've seen today?" the Sergeant asked.

"That's the one," Mr. King said.

"Wait right here. Don't anyone go away," Sergeant Collins said. Then he walked out of the store.

"What's going on here?" Lucky asked.

"We just have to wait. Sergeant Collins said he would be right back," Ricky said.

"I don't know why I have to stay here. I haven't done anything," Lucky said.

"Here he comes," Tom said.

Just then Sergeant Collins came back into the store. But he wasn't alone.

Tom, Ricky, and Mr. King all looked at Sergeant Collins. The man with him looked just like Lucky. He had red hair. He even had a red shirt.

"Look at that!" Ricky said.

Then Mr. King said, "What's this all about?"

The man with him looked just like Lucky.

Tom and Ricky looked at the two men with the red hair.

"I can't tell one from the other," Tom said.

"They're twins," Sergeant Collins said.

"Please tell me what's going on," Mr. King said.

"Sam told me two men came by to see him. They said they had good tires to sell. They said Sam could buy them. They said they didn't want much money," Sergeant Collins said.

"Sam at the gas station?" Tom asked.

"That's right. Sam told me about the woman who had two missing tires. Then these two came to his station. They had two good tires to sell him," Sergeant Collins said.

"Did you know they were twins?" Ricky asked.

"No. Sam wasn't sure. He just saw one of them. The other stayed in the car," Sergeant Collins said.

"When did you begin to think they were twins?" Tom asked.

"When you told me about seeing Lucky so many times. Then I knew something was wrong," Sergeant Collins said.

"But why did one stay in the store all the time?" Tom asked.

Sergeant Collins turned to the twins. "Do you want to answer that?" he asked.

"We're not saying anything," Lucky said.

"I know why," Ricky said.

"Let's hear it," Mr. King said.

"Lucky talked a lot to Tom and me. That way he could say he was in the store. If anyone said a man with red hair was around, he could say he was here," Ricky said.

"And the other one took tires off of the cars out there," Tom said.

"That's right," Sergeant Collins said.

"I'll take these two men with me. I'll see that all those people get their tires back. I think the tires are in the red car," Sergeant Collins said.

Sergeant Collins left with the twins.

"All that red. It really made them stand out," Tom said.

"That's what they wanted. They thought it would help them," Ricky said.

"It almost worked. They didn't think anyone would see one in the store and one in the lot at the same time," Mr. King said.

"Isn't it about time to close the store?" Tom asked.

"Yes, it is. And I'm going to pay you both right now. You'll have money to buy that bike you want, Ricky," Mr. King said.

Mr. King took the boys over to the money box. "I'm paying you more than I said I would. That's for being a big help to me. I think you can get to Mr. Ward's store before he closes," Mr. King said.

"Thanks very much," Ricky said.

Ricky jumped on Tom's bike. They were on their way to see Mr. Ward.

"You know what?" Tom called out.

"What?" Ricky asked.

"We only knew the name of one of the twins," Tom said.

"Well, whatever his name was, I think we were the lucky ones today," Ricky said.